PASSAGE

bi Anca bower

PASSAGE

COPYRIGHT © 2015 BIANCA BOWERS

Published by Paperfields Press

Book Cover Design by Bianca Bowers

Book Cover Art © Anna Ismagilova (Shutterstock ID 1539970361)

All rights reserved. No part of this publication may be reproduced, distributed, or transmitted in any form or by any means, including photocopying, recording, or other electronic or mechanical methods, without the prior written permission of the publisher, except in the case of brief quotations embodied in critical reviews and certain other noncommercial uses permitted by copyright law. For permission requests, email the publisher: "Attention: Permissions"
info@paperfieldspress.com
www.paperfieldspress.com

ISBN-13: 978-0-9942404-1-5

EPub ISBN-13: 978-0-9942404-2-2

Third Edition January 2020

For my grandmothers, biological and other:
Anne, Wilhelmina, and Freda.

Acknowledgements

The author wishes to acknowledge the following:

THE EDITORS of the following journal where this poem originally appeared:

SHOT GLASS JOURNAL (MUSE PIE PRESS): "She leaves her soul in the stairwell".

MY HUSBAND AND CHILDREN for their unconditional support.

Contents

Prelude	3

RESTLESS ☀

Seduce my restless heart	7
Mess	9
Plagiarist	12
A Monster of Authenticity	13
Brisbane breathes	14
Identity	15
Chamber	16
Trapped	17

RESTLESS ☾

Lotus in the Sahara	21
Los Angeles	23
In the End	24
I hunt the shadow	26
She leaves her soul in the stairwell	28

FRICTION ☀

America	31
Immigrant	33
My face runs through the park	35
Fairytale	36

Conditioning	38
I see a woman's reflection—	39
Envy	40
As if love was ever enough	41
Resurrection or Burial	42
A dissected heart	44

FRICTION ☾

Fickle	47
Flowers and Lies	48
I sail on the wind	49
I've fallen	50
Ghosts	51
I	52
Gargoyle Moon	53

REFLECTION ☀

The Memory of Water	57
England, my England	59
A red helicopter	60
The Devil's Courtyard	61
I sit between pines	63
Six Thousand Nautical Miles	64
September	65
Teenagers graffiti the trees	67

Complicate me	68
If I was a map	69

REFLECTION ☾

Belonging	75
1920	76
Groundhog	77
I hid inside a piano	78
The ravens are everywhere	79
My heart collects dust	80
I want to swap my feet	81
Rain	82

PASSAGE

Behind glass	85
I'm travelling to the clouds	86
Palace	87
I imagine that I'm a girl again	89
Seventeen	90
We'll fly in pairs	91
A stranger to belonging	92
Let us touch the dawn	93
My ghost beckons me	94
Caterpillar	95
NOTES	97
ABOUT THE AUTHOR	99

Prelude

My feet were fused with a 7-lane highway
My spine, dismantled;
a map of bones with no instruction.

The pith of my existence, banished
to the crepuscule
while my hands waged war
left and right

I made futile attempts—
split the heavens with questions
turned idols into gods
placed the moon on my windowsill
surrendered the sun to strangers

but, the owl light hooted still

Without wings or feet I resolved
to sojourn in twilight's palm and eavesdrop
ritualistically, on the susurration of duality, until

I deciphered its tongue when
the highway mouth met the lip
of the sky

Releasing a flock of ravens
into a new dawn.

Restless

Seduce my restless heart

untie me
I am stained yellow
from yesterday's sunshine

we draw together
like curtains at dusk
shed our skin
at dawn

We belong to yesterday
but cannot be discarded
yet

blindly instinctive
we inch toward the sky
like caterpillars

these parallel lines
travel together
but never meet

Perhaps my love for squares
has estranged me from my own heart

I am restless
I am restless
I am restless

Mess

The goldfish died this morning, I
blame myself
lie to my kids
assure that I will bury
versus bin, I

feel the cold snowball
add another layer
keep moving
compartmentalising is my PhD, I

ignore whites, darks, colours
overflowing laundry
baskets will wait like patients
awaiting treatment, I

do not take precedence
today the dishwasher is gridlocked
while repairmen go walkabout
outback, weeds grow at the rate of words, I

spy my manuscript upon the desk
but writing is as lucrative as motherhood
vacuuming deserves greater urgency, I

spring clean in winter, attempt
to alleviate baggage—
donate
recycle—but it only awards
five extra breaths, I

am counting to ten again
my phone is buzzing
Though I've switched
paper bills to email they still win
the mind game, I

scrape yolk off the pine table
sweep crumbs and ants
from terracotta tiles
blot a rogue tear with my sleeve, I

admit that I'm failing
to clean this mess
but cannot entertain
a pity party, I

put my self on
the back burner of time
prepare to cart kids, assist with homework
cook dinner, tend to emotions, I

am a family home in a treelined suburb—
two kids
one husband
minus, one goldfish.

Plagiarist

If I could go back
I would not plant a forest
from roots of trauma

for the future is pre-destined—
felling of trees,
one by one until,
I am nothing
more than a plagiarist.

A monster of authenticity

is imprisoned in my chest

With its claws
it scratches at bars of deception
With its teeth
it gnaws truthful titbits

My chest no longer holds its weight
Ribs break, one by one, as it
hoists itself
squeezes my feeble heart, until
my chest is a pressurised cabin
breathing is dying
piecemeal

This monster of authenticity
has an appetite for freedom,
and I can no longer ignore
its eloquent demands

Brisbane breathes

but my lungs gasp

for fresh air. Australia
is not my bedfellow

Yet here we lie;
de facto partners
unwilling to institutionalise
                    our union.

Identity

My identity is pegged
to a clothesline

My value drips
like a leaky tap

My intellect is bleached
like cistern and sink

My memory of desire
is a smudge of dust on glass

My responsibility hems me in
to margins of domesticity

A territory without sovereignty
with the responsibility of Artemis
and no more respect than Eve

Chamber

I stand at the feet
of a cracked sky
counting
its broken clouds

I sit at the kitchen table
writing
sonnets to mediocrity

I shelter inside a question mark
watch the moon
dwarf
my bedroom window

My body trembles
inside this chamber
My voice echoes
inside this box

Trapped

I am trapped;
a parasol of honey
in a sky full of ants.

I have drowned the sun
ignited the rain
fished stars from sewers
tasted bittersweet
dichotomy

Now, I tuck the moon into my pocket
lay a snow-trap for the climactic storm
that will end the endless summer
before it burns the clouds alive.

Restless

Lotus in the Sahara

I grow melancholy
when my heart travels
away from love,

when it hides behind clocks
and plummets into wasteland.

I grow restless
when the moon hatches
from its shell,

when hunger strikes
like midnight.

I grow distant
without the love
of earthlings,

when dream trees bloom
from my torso,
but never reach the sky.

I grow melancholy

when I grow and grow,
but never bloom:

a lotus in the Sahara.

Los Angeles

I yearn to shed this city
like superfluous skin

I snake up Mt Coot-tha
to Brisbane's crown
and imagine Mulholland;
the city of angels in my lap.

Los Angeles glitters
like a sea of lights;
luring monotony
with attractions of artifice,
cloning flocks of helicopters,
with no reason to migrate.

Is this really what my heart wants?

In the end

It was all about time
in the end

after the rain fell
wisteria enveloped the trellis

We whispered our love
under the moon's hips

when love was our reason
each day blossomed at night

An imaginary love, it was not…

even after the rain short-circuited
electric hands

after we pressed words into our mouths
and choked on the bones

after the rain
washed us away
and exiled us back to the sun

to burn,
day in
and day out,

without the anticipation of night.

In the end
it was all about time.

I hunt the shadow

I turn my palms toward clouds
and lean
inside forests I hunt the shadow
that ridicules the trees
and reveres the sky

I hunt the shadow of hungry
vampires in the infancy of ambition
insatiable, upon resurrection, emancipated
from a heart pumping blood
and bleeding

I hunt the shadow, red
admiral against a metamorphic sky
sailing above pines and gums
on the grace of impeccable timing

I hunt the shadow, forgotten
in a fossilised forest, autumn
is indifferent and time
skips backwards

I drive against time

to elevated planes
to hunt the shadow that soars
above clouds and falls without warning
to settle in the comfort of trees

She leaves her soul in the stairwell

at dusk.

Folds her petticoat heart
before the snow-capped raven
serenades the moon.

Padlocks her tongue
while the storm gathers emotion

Slips into a bath of disinfectant
to scrub the subterranean scars

And,
when her skin catches its breath,

she secures her anxiety to a moth's wings,
and watches it flee the night.

Friction

America
For Ezra and Allen

America
I have dreamed inside your belly
since my first moving image
You were the playground to my inner child
the stars in my telescope...
I have yearned for you like a twin
separated at birth
and yet
our reunion seems unlikely

America
I have sojourned inside your belly
long enough to suspend my Hollywood belief
Travelled the arc of marriage and divorce
until my catharsis was complete
and I emerged from the pupa of Jefferson
into the mosquito hawk of Ginsberg—
unable to deny the philosophical conundrum
you were becoming

America
I have aged inside your belly

thinking that dogma couldn't grow
from your democratic roots
Only to witness it burgeon into the strength of an oak
You have encased that hallowed scroll in the dungeon
of absolute power
and disfigured its face beyond recognition

America
I have howled inside your belly
Even your mouthpiece has lost its freedom
only one voice can be heard above the din of Tinseltown theatrics—
the voice of fear mongering.
You have knowingly peddled pills to your children
and they have patriotically swallowed the blues
resigned themselves to the matrix
of merchants and modifiers

America
I have shriveled inside your belly
I wrote about you once
with the romanticism of Shakespeare
Now, I must exile those youthful manuscripts
—like Pound
and trust the doubt of Thomas
until your next reincarnation.

Immigrant
For the immigrants around the world

I am an immigrant
collecting years like postage stamps
a countdown to belonging...

My immigrant skin remembers
its motherland;
my roots
haunt me at night.

My immigrant skin is visible
when I speak;
my inflection labels me
as foreign.

My immigrant skin longs to belong
but cannot deny its destiny;
to be appraised
and never evolve past prototype.

My immigrant skin does not belong
here nor there;
it is misshapen and superfluous

to the jigsaw.

I don't know how to tell you, Australia
that my collection is 8 years strong,
yet my immigrant skin blushes
with foreign pretence.

I'm talking to you, Australia
I'm asking you to look at me,
to listen to me.
I am an immigrant
with much to contribute:
diversity,
compassion,
stories.

I chose YOU
over my motherland
and my story
is your story now.

My face runs through the park

You can pick me
from a voice line-up
and slip a mask
into my party bag

but I'm less Austen
and more Buchowski
than you can handle

My face runs through the park
barefoot
and I pursue boundaries
like a highway bandit

I'm a heavyweight boxer
and I'll relish a collision
with pseudo smiles

I'll neither dye my tongue
nor bury my voice
and I'll conform
as much as Chuck

Fairytale

If I could
blink and pause
I would sacrifice love

I nominated love
when my heart was a fairytale
and now
love is the villain

Now, love has plunged a sword
between my ribs
and my heart is bleeding rainbows

This love has labeled me, it lives
to siphon colour
to straighten curves
to define what is nameless

But
it is not the lone survivor

This love is at war
with a dragon

A dragon who lives beyond
this chapter of stereotype

A dragon
who grows in my chest
who feasts on love's leftovers
who hungers for battle

A dragon
who approaches adulthood
with a belly full of rainbows

Conditioning

Oh, cruel conditioning
that tattoos my thoughts
with colourless ink

Even now
with years in stockpile
I find myself
tripping
over my own intuition

Oh, twisted words
like gnarled roots in the garden
My stories are weeds
that must be poisoned

Oh, loyalty
impermanent as midnight

Oh, love
as thorny as a rose

Distance, is all that's left—
mileage
the only remedy.

I see a woman's reflection—

Her resignation to limitation
infects me
Her willingness to compromise sits
behind the wheel of my choices

I see a woman's reflection—
Three month's away from crisis
with her borrowed ribs
Her skin,
with its lines, racing
toward failure.

I see a woman's reflection—
Still failing to claim
her identity
Still swallowing
her voice
Still limping
towards impotence.

I see a woman's reflection—
But I will not look away this time
This time, I will not blink.

Envy

She drives her beat up Ford
with a fag in her hand
like the future is someone else's
bookmark

Failing to see her rebellion
for what it is

Insects and snails
possess better instincts
in a puddle of rain
than you, sweet child

Adult in name only
you rest inside carved out apples
that long since fell off the tree

You will wait in vain,
destroy the orchard
with envy

If only spring could save you.

As if love was ever enough

to milk flowers
to extract beauty from anger

As if griffin wings were
delicate enough
to preserve a heart
ferocious enough
to make it flutter

As if expectations would never be
mapped
onto a skin's topography
battered
during tempests

As if
love was indestructible
time was a defence
context factored into history

As if love was ever enough to
survive a choice
that carries too much cargo
to jettison

Resurrection or Burial

I carry the cadaver
of our relationship
drape broken ribs
and torn flesh
around my fattened shoulders

A martyr
demanding you to feed
on your own carrion

The mirror that has reflected
superiority for decades
is shattered
my reflection pierced
with shards of truth
that denial has feasted upon
like a predatory beast
since my damaged heart
bled into yours

Reality limps
from its pitiful cage;
aimless
confused

married to its conditioning

I've unburdened my shoulders
of a cadaver's weight
Now, it lies at my feet
twitching from the mutilation
I have inflicted

I have only two choices:
Resurrection or Burial.

Dissected heart

I have thought too much about you
preoccupied my hands with surgery

A dissected heart
is all that's left—
bloody hands
a reminder of my failure
to love you.

Friction

Fickle

A tarmac horizon
stretches its legs
beneath

fickle feet that itch
to kick
a spineless life

The sky unleashes the moon
I swallow it before
it decomposes

A raven breaks loose
from my chest

Flowers and Lies

float
in a sickle-shaped bath
Cheekbones play the piano
beneath a watery shawl

I can filter the sun here
drag it below the steam
alter it with gauze
and rosemary

I can anchor the harvest moon here
swill poetic mysticism
postpone my tidal heart

I can haunt the labyrinth here
watch flowers and lies
self-destruct

I sail on the wind

with a piano in my chest
ribs tapping a sweet melody

I search
  for a saviour in the sky
scour
  caves for clues
only to chase
  butterflies up mountains
flick flies
  with a horses tail.

I tend to the truth
  before it speeds away
tailgate shadows
  that never blink
Admit
  I cannot level trees with my ego
  nor cut the electricity to your soul
  when burning is not a choice in the forest

I've fallen

into freedom's arms
but barely scratched
reality's face

I've travelled
to a standstill with my heart
in my hands

I'm sinking
in ordinary quicksand—
my heart
my head
a muted melody

If my heart is my compass
then I am lost

Ghosts

A leaf of notes
lives on the windowsill

The window where ghosts glimmer;

pressing their boney faces
against glass
like cold exclamations.

I

My bookcase brims with stories
My photographs haemorrhage memories
But, I
am a stranger

I
whisper
at sensory edges
of a submerged life

I
knock
behind bolted doors

In between the silence
In between the seasons
In between the rhythm
In between the currents

I
exist.

Gargoyle Moon

A naked sky surrenders
teardrops on raven hats
congregate
in her garden of passion
flowers climb tombstones

Rain splashes
in graveyard fountains
Its scent flooding
the woodland pocket where
she shares earth with worms
who use her cavities without permission

Squeaky soles remind her
leftover skin
of a power-hungry night
when she rested her chin
on his shoulder. Mesmerised
by an undulating ribbon
of bats flying past
the gargoyle moon.

Reflection

The Memory of Water

A dusty blue boat
—red, lopsided smile
peeling, like sunburnt skin—
capsized in tall green grass
behind a little white house

Motorless and damaged, but afloat,
on the memory of water.

The neighbour's house
—always bathed in sunshine—
so enchanting
through a peephole in weathered timber fence

The tall woman
—in a rainbow dress and straw hat—
hummed like a honey bee
adrift amongst sunflowers

I dreamed of her on dark nights
dreamed about belonging to sunshine

Even at five

I had more in common with that capsized boat
than the Summer woman

Me and my childhood boat
—flotsam and jetsam—
but
only one of us lived
with the memory of water.

England, my England

or is it someone else's?

Overcast skies smile in my mind
Sunshine scowls in my face
Still, is weather enough
to change direction?

A city with a pulse may never sleep
yet dreaming comes so easily down under
Is it one
or the other
that causes insomnia?

Is youth possible in an ageing city?

A red helicopter

sleeps
in the woods children frolic
on the arms of fallen gums

Blue sky searches for clouds
while I search prisms
of dappled light

Towers with red signals
communicate enigmatically
Laughing kookaburras congregate like old friends
Stones hide secrets in the creek

Everything here, besides me
belongs.

The Devil's Courtyard

The wind powders my cheek
with its willowy breath
Heaven exists in my open palm
yet I stand in the devil's courtyard

where turquoise sunshine
romances my geographic memory
and the geometry of a future
haemorrhages
beneath the weight of calculus

I sprawl my colonial limbs
over swamp cypress roots
knowing
that my familiarity with reptiles is futile
that the fantasy cannot exist
beyond my sultry skin

Whenever the clouds capitulate
I dream of a preferable reflection
But, that fibreglass lake is a mirror
fraught with allergy
destined to splinter

into fractals of existence

If I pluck the feathers from my words
and feed myself to you in slivers
your palate may salivate and smile
but purple pretence will not upholster
my bird-less nest.

Floating towards safety
is a paradoxical vessel
(to which I have no membership)
Tunneling elongates time.
Will mercy kill time for me
until time is bloodless beside the vein of reward?

Windows
can be enigmatic at dusk
and sheets of colour at dawn
Ancient blossoms need not sleep
amongst fossilised branches forever

I sit between pines

autumn and winter

where Japanese slate cools
and birds dip wings into the falls

Running water
narrates my solitude
Children's voices keep me present

Conifers grow in tiers
near the waterfall—
tall enough to reach
raven's nest.

Six Thousand Nautical Miles

I find peace amongst tombs—
where nature reclaims bones
and crows prey
on leftover dreams

Memories, as old as rust,
reverberate
from this diamond-shaped
wire
that holds my spine
like my grandmother did
Memories as old as her ashes—
psychic fragments congregate
here

on this bench
in a Toowong cemetery
six thousand nautical miles
from Durban—the birthplace
of a journey.

September

Give me a wildflower to
remember
how desire lit the night

Hand in hand, on a September's day,
we watched damselflies hover
in a shaft of light;
magic coursed our veins.

My confidence had a lifespan
of morning dew, but
my heart was invincible;
oblivious to the ocean it was crossing.

Annotated secrets, penciled
into dog-eared journals
that contained more truth
than fingerprints

Celestial bodies could not stem the tides
that drew us together
and pulled us apart

How love echoes under the waves

where we drowned

And all we can do
is sink our lips
into September

Teenagers graffiti the trees

with their love
Yet I cannot find

a single leaf of passion
to clasp against my heart
like a resuscitation paddle

Complicate me

until I am unattainable;
a pedestal of lace
to a lazy eye.

Porcelain attempts
will age our youthful hands
and strip our eyes of diamonds

A shatterproof existence
flickers
like a silhouette
on a slender path

If I was a map

I'd be coffee stained
and cigarette burnt
dog-eared
and footprinted
full of locations I never want to return to

I drive between suburbs
treelined streets
and trailer parks
trying to eliminate my anxiety
the mutant butterfly
at my core
that won't stop flapping
whose only intent is to cause a stir

I ache to stop
but there are roadblocks and detours
and hellish traffic
It seems fate has followed me here too
—intent to harass and stalk
until I break
down and do
its bidding

Only I've forgotten what that is
and I can't for the love of God
or the life of me
remember
Why I'm here, or how I got here
or what I want after this is over
after the last brick has been removed
from my condemned walls

Eventually, I see it
a park
stop
but it's just my luck to find
it fenced up with keep out signs
warning me off
like a dilapidated house
but there are no buildings here
only trees

I'm looking for a saviour
all the while knowing
that nobody will save me
because I don't deserve to be saved
because I'm a sandbox, cemented in
a swimming pool without water
a house without doors

The trees are so peaceful

they breathe for me

and call me closer

but I don't want to be a tree

because trees stay put

they have no feet

and I have been standing still

for too long

My soil is depleted

my nests are empty

and the only sound I hear clearly

is traffic

Reflection

Belonging

is a recurring dream; the sheen of another world on my brow, every time I wake

with a craving for intimacy

that is impossible here,

in this place where I will never belong

in this place where my heart is pickled

in a glass jar on a shelf

behind some books

1920

My heart remembers
black shoelaces and porcelain feet
that never stopped running
toward love

My skin remembers
velvet lips grazing
a glass-beaded dress

My soul remembers
music
filling the bath

Groundhog

I surrender myself to dreams
sleep beneath stars of my own making
map journeys that refuse to relinquish me

searching
for a hairline fracture
in the map parchment that binds
my groundhog existence

I hid inside a piano

until freedom arrived
one enchanting firefly summer

Moving between Dublin and Cornwall
I was never alone on that bench
beneath the beech

I followed Pandora
into a dance hall of flowers
while dreaming with Cleopatra
under a Nile chandelier

We congregated there
—sanity and I—
to escape the world of oxygen

Between the pages
we slipped and ran
until letters and words
were breathless

The ravens are everywhere

I turn

They follow me
yet I cannot get close enough
        to smell their feathers
        or touch their singed beaks

I try to blend with the pines
plant cones at my feet
turn my hands into vines...

but the ravens flee
my earthly smell;
their wings are not for sale.

My heart collects dust

between seasons, hibernates
in the snow

I curse the idle light
that paints the walls red
at night

Morning dew means nothing
without sunshine
with expectations that collapse like feathers

I hear the murder before dawn
breaks beyond the gate
and strain to decipher the wisdom
of shadows
from last eve's moonlight

I want to swap my feet

Raven perches on a wire
Unperturbed
by rain driving all
undercover

With wet wings and beak turned skyward
she remains
grateful

I want to swap my feet for trunks
after all
imbibe the sky's emotion

    watch my ankles sprout new roots
    hear my voice chime with cicadas' chorus
    feel flowers blooming from my fingertips

Rain

The sky is an ocean
at high tide
The wind
a vengeful banshee

Lightning swaggers across water
electrifying trees

I am not afraid

This
is life at full throttle
It howls my name
until I answer it
barefoot
like Raven on her wire

Driving rain
raining a refrain

Remember your lion heart
Courage won't break your spine
Swap your feet for wings

Passage

Behind glass

A slice of orange heart
is tangled in floral vines

I wait to bloom
behind glass

I'm travelling to the clouds

in a four wheel drive
the back seat whistles and snores
with every twist of the mountain spine

freckled trees lean
to the east, gorge
on sunshine

forest feet rest
in moss
branches point like arrows
to dragonflies zigzagging glitter
paths in the sky

South Pine river meanders
through the goat track
where 25 acres of dreams
spring to life

Palace

I am so much more
than a palace of bones and skin
Yet, I'm trapped

in the corridors of my own grandeur
broken mirrors busy
my hands with tweezers and glue
but rarely reflect the beauty of my surroundings

I've accumulated decades of days
in this temporal palace
Yet, mystery presides

Hidden tunnels hum
below exposed skin
memories understand more about me
than I do of them

I live here
in a home of strangers
and friends
with sundial and moon
instruments

Windows with views
and basements with walls—
all have felt like home.

I don't know how...

but I trust the uncertainty
of dreams that carry me
along canals
like a ferry in Venice
For there is still so much
still so much
to fill a lifetime
of books
if I wish

I am so much more
than a palace of bones and skin.

I imagine that I'm a girl again

I imagine that I'm Emily...

I wander the moors
and surrender my winter skin
to the bleak sky

I distil isolation
and discover a crocus of creativity

I stumble across a primrose path
and lose my virginity

>   When I find my voice
>   it muzzles the lark's chorus

>   >   I rival the wind
>   >   atop the thundering crag
>   >   and pry Heathcliff from my heart

My roots shrivel below the heath
but harebells bloom from my fingertips

Seventeen

I rose
before demand woke up

With a warm mug in hand
I watched the sun stretch
Counted seventeen
pairs of wings before
blue tigers migrated
toward misty Mount Glorious

The air was new;
nothing belonged to yesterday.

My heart seams split
inside the magpies chorus
The sound of tapping
filled the room

We'll fly in pairs

toward the pines
shelter in the clouds
my love

Can you smell the trees?
The butterflies have hatched
My heart blooms
in the forest

A stranger to belonging

My anxiety to belong
has skewed my perspective
but there is more to belonging
than meets

the eye
of the beholder, like beauty
has a skein of influence

when life is weighed on a merchant's scale

I am a stranger
to belonging
I know that now
Acceptance holds my hand
and squeezes

Let us touch the dawn

Here we are
confessions apart

We escaped the cyclone
this time
the damage is but a figment
of time

The years cannot strip us
of roses nor carve us
into wrinkles
if we fall on our fear
and rise in truth
if we sever the umbilical
from the belly of life

Let us touch the dawn
with naked fingers
and open hearts
that beat in the face of dogma

My ghost beckons me

into the misty pines
and I follow
like autumn

The clouds dip their fingers
into my thoughts
I fill the sky
with poetry

A native I have never been
not even in my birthplace
but the forest hugs my ankles
until I glow—
like a lamp draped
in damask silk

The snow may never arrive
but I have found a way
to breathe

Caterpillar

Though my head casts shadows over the city
I am no skyscraper
And though a river runs through my veins
I am yet to meet the ocean

For now, intention skips
west toward hourglass mountains
a tidal wave engulfs
nostalgia

At worst, I am a forest
who has sacrificed a tree
but I am not a tree
who has sacrificed its roots

As long as I am made
of blood and ribs
I can build a life
with bone and marrow

I am not a dream

A synthesised mind
hums in rhythm

with a chest of vibrating bees

My caterpillar spine
escapes
its chrysalis

Notes

AMERICA is inspired by two great rebel poets, Allen Ginsberg and Ezra Pound. In particular, Ginsberg's poems, *America* and *Howl*. Both influential and controversial figures, Ginsberg and Pound were not afraid to express their opinions and interrogate the status quo.

IMMIGRANT is a revised version of Immigrant Skin (previously published in Death and Life, 2014).

MY FACE RUNS THROUGH THE PARK

There is a deliberate typo in this poem. Can you spot it, and can you guess its significance?
Visit my blog to read all about it:

https://biancabowers.com/the-deliberate-typo-in-passage-unveiled-is-it-worth-taking-a-creative-risk-in-web-2-0-era/

A RED HELICOPTER is a wink to William Carlos Williams' THE RED WHEELBARROW.

I HID INSIDE A PIANO makes reference to the authors I read in my teens, Rosamunde Pilcher and Maeve Binchy.

I IMAGINE THAT I'M A GIRL AGAIN was inspired by this quote:

"I wish I were a girl again, half savage and hardy, and free..."

~ Emily Brontë from Wuthering Heights.

LET US TOUCH THE DAWN is a wink to Denise Levertov's "What wild dawns there were".

About the Author

Bianca Bowers is a South African-born, Australian-based writer who has also lived in the UK and New Zealand. She holds a BA in English and Film/TV/Media Studies and her poems have appeared in film, print anthologies, and online journals over the last twenty years.

Bianca is the author of *Cape of Storms*, as well as five poetry books. Her second novel, *Three Hearts*, is due in 2020.

You can find Bianca at:
https://www.biancabowers.com

To leave a review, please visit:
https://amazon.com/author/biancabowers
https://www.goodreads.com/BiancaBowersAuthor